Images of
CHELTENHAM

ERIC FRANKS ARPS

SUTTON PUBLISHING LIMITED

Sutton Publishing Limited
Phoenix Mill · Thrupp · Stroud
Gloucestershire · GL5 2BU

First published 2000

Copyright © Eric Franks, 2000

British Library Cataloguing in Publication Data
A catalogue record for this book is available from the
British Library.

ISBN 0-7509-2472-1

Typeset in 10.5/13.5 Photina.
Typesetting and origination by
Sutton Publishing Limited.
Printed and bound in England
by J.H. Haynes & Co. Ltd, Sparkford.

*To my wife Dorothy and to the memory of
my friend Pat Christie*

CONTENTS

Introduction   5

Acknowledgements   6

1. The Environs of the Parish Church   7

2. In and Around the Promenade   13

3. Montpellier   51

4. High Street and Beyond   61

5. Fairview   73

6. Pittville   79

7. Here and There   87

8. Autumn   99

9. Winter   113

10. After Dark   125

Introduction

I grew up in the industrial Midlands, in a location that owed its origin to the Great Northern Railway establishing there a railway depot, the second largest in the region. Modest red brick villas rubbed shoulders with streets of small terraced houses. In spite of the ever-present engine smoke, Nottingham lace was by far the most popular curtain material and no parlour would have been considered complete without an aspidistra in the window.

It was a friendly close-knit community in which to live and work, but I had itchy feet when I was young and they brought me eventually to Cheltenham, to the editorial department of Ed. J Burrow, publishers of maps, street plans and guides. I was immediately impressed by the change of environment, the beauty of the Regency architecture, the wealth of lovely trees and the atmosphere of seedy gentility but it took me some time to get used to the slower tempo of everyday life. Soon after I arrived I chanced to meet a tutor from St Paul's College who had been one of my schoolteachers. He said he was pleased to see me in Cheltenham but warned me not to stay too long as it was a dangerous place for an ambitious young man. I soon realised what he meant but I have no regrets at having ignored his advice.

I hope the photographs which gave me so much pleasure to take between 1937 and 1953 will revive nostalgic memories for the not-so-young and for others a realisation of how greatly Cheltenham has changed during the past fifty to sixty years.

Acknowledgements

I would like to express warmest thanks to my friends Cyril and Jean Bint, Steven Blake, Jim Stevenson and Peter Thorns for their invaluable help and advice in the preparation of this book.

Promenade fantasy.

1

The Environs of the Parish Church

Where better to begin than in the environs of the parish church? The pawnbroker on the corner of Well Walk kindly allowed me to take this view of the spire from his first floor window.

After 1941 a united choir served both St Matthew's and the parish church.

Heeding the 'hurry bell', or perhaps you would call it the 'parson's bell'.

The church cat kept a wary eye on passers-by.

In those days the neatly kept churchyard provided a peaceful retreat from the noise and bustle of the nearby High Street.

Well Walk.

Chester Walk was a quiet by-way before the Library was extended to house the music and children's departments.

Fortunately the County Court lions were spared when so much of the town's ironwork was sacrificed for the war effort.

I was lucky to have my camera handy when normally drab Clarence Street was suddenly transformed after a summer shower.

Something of the unique character of the Promenade disappeared when Cavendish House was modernized. Concerted efforts to preserve the best features of the Regency frontage failed and 'Cav' became just another store.

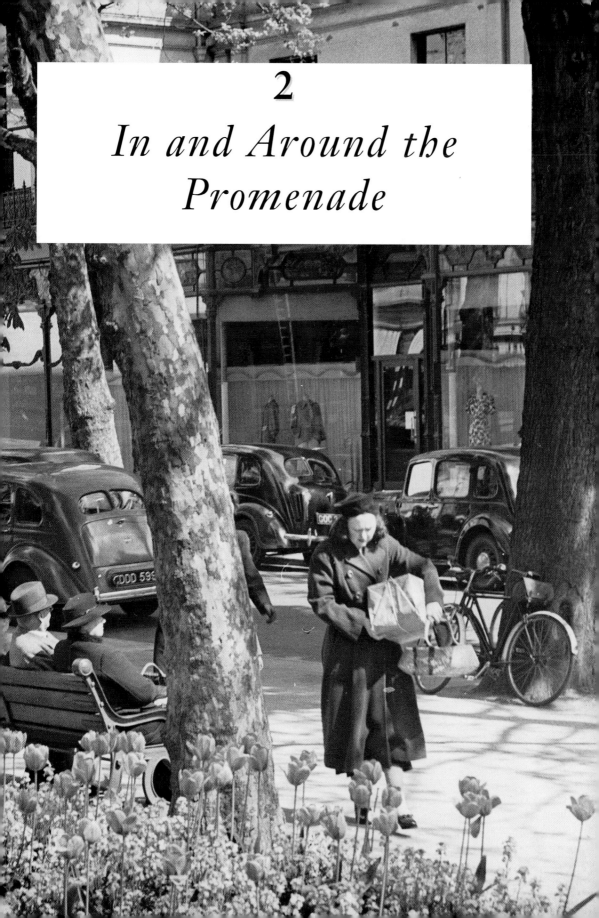

2
In and Around the Promenade

Before the post office moved to its present obscure location in the High Street, it was the hub of the town centre and a popular rendezvous: 'Meet you outside the GPO'.

The fading white bands round the lamp posts and trees were reminders of the wartime blackout.

Robbie, the paper seller with his monotonous cry of 'Echo, Echo', was a permanent feature of the Promenade scene for more than forty years. The placard referred to Hitler's annexation of Austria in March 1938.

The annual display of tulips made it a pleasure to post a letter, until the flower beds were removed in the interest of improving access to the post office.

Salvage bins remained a necessary eyesore for several years after the war ended.

The overhanging branches of the chestnut trees provided a perfect frame for the Municipal Offices.

'Now take Cheltenham for instance. . . .'

I offer no apology for including images of people watching the world go by, for they express more vividly than words the leisurely atmosphere of the town before it was abruptly shattered by the outbreak of war.

Before the avenue of ageing chestnut trees had to be felled, the sight of the blossom from the steps of the Municipal Offices was unforgettable.

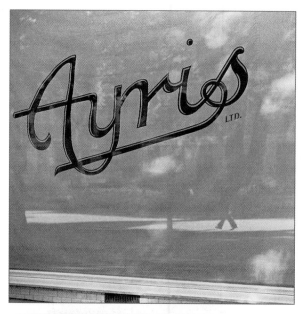

Not just an image of a shop window with the blind down, but surviving evidence of the deep social divide that emerged in the eighteenth and early nineteenth centuries with the discovery of the medicinal springs that resulted in Cheltenham becoming a fashionable spa town.

Early closing day in the town was Wednesday, but in the Promenade and Montpellier the shops closed at one o'clock on Saturday and the larger ones drew their blinds.

The flower seller set up his stall outside Nixon's china shop on Saturday mornings when the Promenade was the place in which to be seen. In the afternoon he moved to the High Street.

A young lady tripped along in the spring sunshine . . .

. . . and a bobby proceeded.

Few passers-by appeared to notice the unusual Regency frontage of Belgrave House at the corner of the Promenade and Imperial Square.

The Spa Harp Trio, better known as the Thirsty Three, had a police permit to perform at certain places in the town, including the Cadena. When I invited them to come over to the sunny side of the Prom to be photographed they refused, but the sight of half-a-crown quickly changed their minds and they obliged on the understanding that they merely posed and didn't actually play.

During periods of hot weather, when the atmosphere beneath the Promenade trees became unbearably stifling, Neptune was a star attraction.

Fans of Humphrey Bogart studying the programme at the Regal cinema, since replaced by RoyScot House.

Royal Well before it was desecrated by the ugly concrete bus shelters – now themselves replaced.

Town bus services started from Royal Well Road.

The shrill sound of young voices in Imperial Square heralded the children from Nazareth House in Bath Road on their way to St Gregory's RC School in Knapp Road.

The Ladies' College pupils were on their way to school from Farnley Lodge boarding house, now the YMCA, in Vittoria Walk.

n those days the pupils' entrance to the college was in St George's Road.

Another way of helping with the homework.

The town centre at the height of
the morning rush hour.

The lengthening shadows of summer evenings outside the New Club were irresistible subjects for my camera.

It would be difficult to imagine the Promenade without the Queen's Hotel, whose imposing Classical façade has dominated Imperial Square since 1838. Residents in the square had a right to enjoy the privacy of the Winter Garden, now known as Imperial Gardens.

Band concerts were a regular feature of the Winter Garden before the bandstand was sold, in 1948, to Bognor Regis – where it is still in use on the seafront.

Spring, summer and autumn in
Imperial Square.

These little girls walked quite alone to their prep school each morning through this then-secluded corner of Imperial Square.

3

Montpellier

Montpellier Walk would have been very quiet on Sunday mornings without the flower seller outside Dodwell's shop.

The swathe of daffodils and narcissi that brought
the first breath of spring to Montpellier more than
sixty years ago still does so today.

The stony stare of the caryatids they passed on their way to school must have remained in the memories of many generations of former Ladies' College pupils.

The Thirsty Three strategically located near to Peter's Bar. No need for a tip this time.

These Ladies' College pupils walking through the Rotunda colonnade were on their way from boarding houses in Suffolk Square. No car runs in those days.

The elegance of the Regency Rotunda contrasts sharply with the Victorian architecture of the Ladies' College.

Montpellier Gardens in spring.

4

The High Street and Beyond

Generations of local boys had passed through the High Street entrance to the Grammar School since it was built in 1889. The school was one of several historic buildings demolished during the widely criticized redevelopment that took place during the 1960s.

Watching the world go by at the corner of St George's Street.

he Old Basket Shop, the oldest secular building in the town, was demolished to provide access to a car park.

n elderly resident of King Street
turning home.

Evening sunshine brought to life the terraced houses in Burton Street and the row of small shops in the Lower High Street.

This photograph of Iddles' fish shop at the corner of Grove Street was taken after the war. The empty shelves, the attitudes of the loungers and the fading posters symbolize for me the mood of exhaustion prevailing at that time.

The superb quality of the fish and chips supplied by Poole's Fish Restaurant, 'top Poole's' as it was called, attracted custom from way beyond the High Street.

Until the arrival of North Sea gas, the district of St Peter's was dominated by the gasworks and polluted by the smog that escaped from the chimney.

Part of the boundary wall remained in Mill Lane: an interesting piece of bricklaying artistry.

his unusual view of St Peter's Church was taken from the gasworks' fuel compound.

A friendly chat opposite the Nag's Head Inn at the corner of Granville Street.

The pawnbroker at the corner of Milsom Street was very security conscious.

5

Fairview

The quiet artisan Regency district of Fairview inspired many pictures before the narrow streets became increasingly cluttered with residents' cars.

Evening sunshine in Fairview Road.

All Saints' School casts
its lengthening shadow
over Fairview streets.

No. 43 Sherborne Street was the home of Frederick Field, the last of a long line of Cheltenham sweeps. I was fortunate to find him sitting on his front doorstep enjoying the evening sunshine. He swept his last chimney in 1950 and his trade sign is now in the local history room of the Museum.

The corner shop still retained its artisan Regency character.

6
Pittville

The decorative ironwork that surmounts Pittville Gates, formerly an entrance to the park.

Where are they now I wonder?
I would like to meet them.

The graceful weeping lime tree is a great deal larger now and is considered to be one of the finest trees in Cheltenham.

Taking the children to feed the swans and mallard was a regular Sunday morning task for many fathers, and indeed grandpas.

A good Sunday morning read under the trees in Pittville Gardens.

Then as now, boating was confined to the western end of the lake.

Silver birch trees at the Pittville Lawn entrance to the park.

7

Here and There

Nelson Lodge, one of three charming Regency villas in Trafalgar Street – where else?

Among the town's wealth of lovely trees the one that most appealed to me was the silver birch, because of the way the cream and black of the bark blended with the stucco and ironwork of the Regency architecture.

The annual cricket week as it was then known, Wally Hammond, Tom Goddard and all returned to the College ground in 1946. The hospitality suites were then somewhat rudimentary.

The 'bicycle stand' in Thirlestaine Road filled up rapidly after the tea interval.

Regency contrasts.

Street signs that point to the past.

Church parade on a foggy morning. Hats and gloves *will* be worn.

Cheltenham College boys in Sandford Road on their way to
morning assembly. Owing to the exorbitant cost and
difficulty in obtaining supplies during the war, boiler suits
were adopted as the school uniform for the duration.

Pupils on their way to Naunton Park primary school. The
box the girl was carrying contained a gasmask, not her
sandwiches.

Parking at the General Hospital was not quite the problem it is now.

Post Regency! At the end of the war temporary houses, officially described as Homes for Heroes, were built t
relieve the acute housing shortage. They quickly became known as prefabs.

Then as now youngsters did their best to hasten the arrival of the conker season.

Misty morning sunshine in September gave advance warning that autumn was not far away.

8

Autumn

Autumn in the Promenade before the chestnut trees had to be felled was quite spectacular.

In October after a night of frost or high wind the Promenade was an unbroken brown carpet until it was disturbed by the early morning traffic.

Not everyone appreciated the beauty of the autumn leaves, and every year there were understandable complaints by elderly residents about the danger of slippery pavements.

'oping with the avalanche was very much a brush and shovel operation.

Harvest Home.

9

Winter

Bare branches and weak sunlight made early winter something of a close season for picture making.

Snow is not a regular visitor to Cheltenham, but the winters of 1940 and 1947 were exceptional and provided me with many opportunities for pictures.

Snowbound streets remained almost deserted.

A dramatic change of climate for the soldier on the Boer War memorial.

Stone cold.

Footprints in the snow in Montpellier Gardens.

The long, drawn-out winter of 1947 ended in slush about the middle of March.

1 0
After Dark

The old-style street lighting brought a mellow glow and an air of mystery to otherwise quite ordinary scenes.

My images of Cheltenham began in the environs of the parish church. I think it is fitting that they should en
with this after-dark photograph of the path through the churchyard.